Hunter's Log

ISBN: 1717238882
ISBN-13: 978-1717238887

Morning or Evening Hunt: *Morning*

Date: *20-Nov-2017*   Location: *Box Blind*

Game: *Whitetail*   Bow/Gun: *Rifle*

Caliber: *30-06 150grain* Scent/Attractant: *Doe in heat*

Weather: *Fresh snow*   Bait: *Sugar beets*

Wind: *Gentle from west* Temperature: *33°*

Sunrise: *7:40*   Sunset: *5:10*

People on Hunt:	Individual Tasks:
Me	*I brought the coffee*
Mikey	*Running call*

About hunt:
This is where you give details and talk about your hunt

Morning or Evening Hunt:

Date: Location:

Game: Bow/Gun:

Caliber: Scent/Attractant:

Weather: Bait:

Wind: Temperature:

Sunrise: Sunset:

People on Hunt: Individual Tasks:

About hunt:

Morning or Evening Hunt:

Date: Location:

Game: Bow/Gun:

Caliber: Scent/Attractant:

Weather: Bait:

Wind: Temperature:

Sunrise: Sunset:

People on Hunt: Individual Tasks:

About hunt:

Morning or Evening Hunt:

Date: Location:

Game: Bow/Gun:

Caliber: Scent/Attractant:

Weather: Bait:

Wind: Temperature:

Sunrise: Sunset:

People on Hunt: Individual Tasks:

About hunt:

Morning or Evening Hunt:

Date: Location:

Game: Bow/Gun:

Caliber: Scent/Attractant:

Weather: Bait:

Wind: Temperature:

Sunrise: Sunset:

People on Hunt: Individual Tasks:

About hunt:

Morning or Evening Hunt:

Date: Location:

Game: Bow/Gun:

Caliber: Scent/Attractant:

Weather: Bait:

Wind: Temperature:

Sunrise: Sunset:

People on Hunt: Individual Tasks:

About hunt:

Morning or Evening Hunt:

Date: Location:

Game: Bow/Gun:

Caliber: Scent/Attractant:

Weather: Bait:

Wind: Temperature:

Sunrise: Sunset:

People on Hunt: Individual Tasks:

________________________   ________________________

________________________   ________________________

________________________   ________________________

________________________   ________________________

________________________   ________________________

________________________   ________________________

About hunt:

____

____

____

____

____

____

____

____

____

____

____

____

____

Morning or Evening Hunt:

Date: Location:

Game: Bow/Gun:

Caliber: Scent/Attractant:

Weather: Bait:

Wind: Temperature:

Sunrise: Sunset:

People on Hunt: Individual Tasks:

About hunt:

Morning or Evening Hunt:

Date: Location:

Game: Bow/Gun:

Caliber: Scent/Attractant:

Weather: Bait:

Wind: Temperature:

Sunrise: Sunset:

People on Hunt: Individual Tasks:

About hunt:

Morning or Evening Hunt:

Date: Location:

Game: Bow/Gun:

Caliber: Scent/Attractant:

Weather: Bait:

Wind: Temperature:

Sunrise: Sunset:

People on Hunt: Individual Tasks:
_______________________|_______________________
_______________________|_______________________
_______________________|_______________________
_______________________|_______________________
_______________________|_______________________
_______________________|_______________________

About hunt:
____
____
____
____
____
____
____
____
____
____
____
____
____
____
____

Morning or Evening Hunt:

Date: Location:

Game: Bow/Gun:

Caliber: Scent/Attractant:

Weather: Bait:

Wind: Temperature:

Sunrise: Sunset:

People on Hunt: Individual Tasks:

About hunt:

Morning or Evening Hunt:

Date: Location:

Game: Bow/Gun:

Caliber: Scent/Attractant:

Weather: Bait:

Wind: Temperature:

Sunrise: Sunset:

People on Hunt: Individual Tasks:

About hunt:

Morning or Evening Hunt:

Date: Location:

Game: Bow/Gun:

Caliber: Scent/Attractant:

Weather: Bait:

Wind: Temperature:

Sunrise: Sunset:

People on Hunt: Individual Tasks:

About hunt:

Morning or Evening Hunt:

Date: Location:

Game: Bow/Gun:

Caliber: Scent/Attractant:

Weather: Bait:

Wind: Temperature:

Sunrise: Sunset:

People on Hunt: Individual Tasks:

About hunt:

Morning or Evening Hunt:

Date: Location:

Game: Bow/Gun:

Caliber: Scent/Attractant:

Weather: Bait:

Wind: Temperature:

Sunrise: Sunset:

People on Hunt: Individual Tasks:

About hunt:

Morning or Evening Hunt:

Date: Location:

Game: Bow/Gun:

Caliber: Scent/Attractant:

Weather: Bait:

Wind: Temperature:

Sunrise: Sunset:

People on Hunt: Individual Tasks:

About hunt:

Morning or Evening Hunt:

Date: Location:

Game: Bow/Gun:

Caliber: Scent/Attractant:

Weather: Bait:

Wind: Temperature:

Sunrise: Sunset:

People on Hunt: Individual Tasks:

About hunt:

Morning or Evening Hunt:

Date: Location:

Game: Bow/Gun:

Caliber: Scent/Attractant:

Weather: Bait:

Wind: Temperature:

Sunrise: Sunset:

People on Hunt: Individual Tasks:

About hunt:

Morning or Evening Hunt:

Date: Location:

Game: Bow/Gun:

Caliber: Scent/Attractant:

Weather: Bait:

Wind: Temperature:

Sunrise: Sunset:

People on Hunt: Individual Tasks:

About hunt:

Morning or Evening Hunt:

Date: Location:

Game: Bow/Gun:

Caliber: Scent/Attractant:

Weather: Bait:

Wind: Temperature:

Sunrise: Sunset:

People on Hunt: Individual Tasks:

About hunt:

Morning or Evening Hunt:

Date: Location:

Game: Bow/Gun:

Caliber: Scent/Attractant:

Weather: Bait:

Wind: Temperature:

Sunrise: Sunset:

People on Hunt: Individual Tasks:

About hunt:

Morning or Evening Hunt:

Date: Location:

Game: Bow/Gun:

Caliber: Scent/Attractant:

Weather: Bait:

Wind: Temperature:

Sunrise: Sunset:

People on Hunt: Individual Tasks:

_______________________   _______________________
_______________________   _______________________
_______________________   _______________________
_______________________   _______________________
_______________________   _______________________
_______________________   _______________________

About hunt:

____
____
____
____
____
____
____
____
____
____
____
____
____
____
____

Morning or Evening Hunt:

Date: Location:

Game: Bow/Gun:

Caliber: Scent/Attractant:

Weather: Bait:

Wind: Temperature:

Sunrise: Sunset:

People on Hunt: Individual Tasks:

About hunt:

Morning or Evening Hunt:

Date: Location:

Game: Bow/Gun:

Caliber: Scent/Attractant:

Weather: Bait:

Wind: Temperature:

Sunrise: Sunset:

People on Hunt: Individual Tasks:

About hunt:

Morning or Evening Hunt:

Date: Location:

Game: Bow/Gun:

Caliber: Scent/Attractant:

Weather: Bait:

Wind: Temperature:

Sunrise: Sunset:

People on Hunt: Individual Tasks:

About hunt:

Morning or Evening Hunt:

Date: Location:

Game: Bow/Gun:

Caliber: Scent/Attractant:

Weather: Bait:

Wind: Temperature:

Sunrise: Sunset:

People on Hunt: Individual Tasks:

About hunt:

Morning or Evening Hunt:

Date: Location:

Game: Bow/Gun:

Caliber: Scent/Attractant:

Weather: Bait:

Wind: Temperature:

Sunrise: Sunset:

People on Hunt: Individual Tasks:

About hunt:

Morning or Evening Hunt:

Date: Location:

Game: Bow/Gun:

Caliber: Scent/Attractant:

Weather: Bait:

Wind: Temperature:

Sunrise: Sunset:

People on Hunt: Individual Tasks:

About hunt:

Morning or Evening Hunt:

Date: Location:

Game: Bow/Gun:

Caliber: Scent/Attractant:

Weather: Bait:

Wind: Temperature:

Sunrise: Sunset:

People on Hunt: Individual Tasks:

About hunt:

Morning or Evening Hunt:

Date: Location:

Game: Bow/Gun:

Caliber: Scent/Attractant:

Weather: Bait:

Wind: Temperature:

Sunrise: Sunset:

People on Hunt: Individual Tasks:

____

____

____

____

____

____

About hunt: ____________________________________

____

____

____

____

____

____

____

____

____

____

____

____

____

____

Morning or Evening Hunt:

Date: Location:

Game: Bow/Gun:

Caliber: Scent/Attractant:

Weather: Bait:

Wind: Temperature:

Sunrise: Sunset:

People on Hunt: Individual Tasks:

About hunt:

Morning or Evening Hunt:

Date: Location:

Game: Bow/Gun:

Caliber: Scent/Attractant:

Weather: Bait:

Wind: Temperature:

Sunrise: Sunset:

People on Hunt: Individual Tasks:

About hunt:

Morning or Evening Hunt:

Date: Location:

Game: Bow/Gun:

Caliber: Scent/Attractant:

Weather: Bait:

Wind: Temperature:

Sunrise: Sunset:

People on Hunt: Individual Tasks:

About hunt:

Morning or Evening Hunt:

Date: Location:

Game: Bow/Gun:

Caliber: Scent/Attractant:

Weather: Bait:

Wind: Temperature:

Sunrise: Sunset:

People on Hunt: Individual Tasks:

About hunt:

Morning or Evening Hunt:

Date: Location:

Game: Bow/Gun:

Caliber: Scent/Attractant:

Weather: Bait:

Wind: Temperature:

Sunrise: Sunset:

People on Hunt: Individual Tasks:

About hunt:

Morning or Evening Hunt:

Date: Location:

Game: Bow/Gun:

Caliber: Scent/Attractant:

Weather: Bait:

Wind: Temperature:

Sunrise: Sunset:

People on Hunt: Individual Tasks:

About hunt:

Morning or Evening Hunt:

Date: Location:

Game: Bow/Gun:

Caliber: Scent/Attractant:

Weather: Bait:

Wind: Temperature:

Sunrise: Sunset:

People on Hunt: Individual Tasks:

About hunt:

Morning or Evening Hunt:

Date: Location:

Game: Bow/Gun:

Caliber: Scent/Attractant:

Weather: Bait:

Wind: Temperature:

Sunrise: Sunset:

People on Hunt: Individual Tasks:
____________________   ____________________
____________________   ____________________
____________________   ____________________
____________________   ____________________
____________________   ____________________
____________________   ____________________

About hunt:
____
____
____
____
____
____
____
____
____
____
____
____
____
____
____

Morning or Evening Hunt:

Date: Location:

Game: Bow/Gun:

Caliber: Scent/Attractant:

Weather: Bait:

Wind: Temperature:

Sunrise: Sunset:

People on Hunt: Individual Tasks:

About hunt:

Morning or Evening Hunt:

Date: Location:

Game: Bow/Gun:

Caliber: Scent/Attractant:

Weather: Bait:

Wind: Temperature:

Sunrise: Sunset:

People on Hunt: Individual Tasks:

About hunt:

Morning or Evening Hunt:

Date: Location:

Game: Bow/Gun:

Caliber: Scent/Attractant:

Weather: Bait:

Wind: Temperature:

Sunrise: Sunset:

People on Hunt: Individual Tasks:

About hunt:

Morning or Evening Hunt:

Date: Location:

Game: Bow/Gun:

Caliber: Scent/Attractant:

Weather: Bait:

Wind: Temperature:

Sunrise: Sunset:

People on Hunt: Individual Tasks:

About hunt:

Morning or Evening Hunt:

Date: Location:

Game: Bow/Gun:

Caliber: Scent/Attractant:

Weather: Bait:

Wind: Temperature:

Sunrise: Sunset:

People on Hunt: Individual Tasks:

About hunt:

Morning or Evening Hunt:

Date: Location:

Game: Bow/Gun:

Caliber: Scent/Attractant:

Weather: Bait:

Wind: Temperature:

Sunrise: Sunset:

People on Hunt: Individual Tasks:

About hunt:

Morning or Evening Hunt:

Date: Location:

Game: Bow/Gun:

Caliber: Scent/Attractant:

Weather: Bait:

Wind: Temperature:

Sunrise: Sunset:

People on Hunt: Individual Tasks:

About hunt:

Morning or Evening Hunt:

Date: Location:

Game: Bow/Gun:

Caliber: Scent/Attractant:

Weather: Bait:

Wind: Temperature:

Sunrise: Sunset:

People on Hunt: Individual Tasks:

About hunt:

Morning or Evening Hunt:

Date: Location:

Game: Bow/Gun:

Caliber: Scent/Attractant:

Weather: Bait:

Wind: Temperature:

Sunrise: Sunset:

People on Hunt: Individual Tasks:

About hunt:

Morning or Evening Hunt:

Date: Location:

Game: Bow/Gun:

Caliber: Scent/Attractant:

Weather: Bait:

Wind: Temperature:

Sunrise: Sunset:

People on Hunt: Individual Tasks:

About hunt:

Morning or Evening Hunt:

Date: Location:

Game: Bow/Gun:

Caliber: Scent/Attractant:

Weather: Bait:

Wind: Temperature:

Sunrise: Sunset:

People on Hunt: Individual Tasks:

About hunt:

Morning or Evening Hunt:

Date: Location:

Game: Bow/Gun:

Caliber: Scent/Attractant:

Weather: Bait:

Wind: Temperature:

Sunrise: Sunset:

People on Hunt: Individual Tasks:

About hunt:

Morning or Evening Hunt:

Date: Location:

Game: Bow/Gun:

Caliber: Scent/Attractant:

Weather: Bait:

Wind: Temperature:

Sunrise: Sunset:

People on Hunt: Individual Tasks:

About hunt: